# let's play
# I SPY
# halloween!

let's play books by
© Little Moon Joy Co

# are you ready to play i spy?

the letters are not in alphabetical order, just like a real game of i spy.

# i spy with my little eye, something beginning with...

## C

# C is for...

# candy

# i spy with my little eye, something beginning with...

# g is for...
## ghost

# i spy with my little eye, something beginning with...

P is for...

pumpkin

# i spy with my little eye, something beginning with...

# b is for...

## bat

# i spy with my little eye, something beginning with...

# V is for...
## vampire

# i spy with my little eye, something beginning with...

# S is for... spider

# i spy with my little eye, something beginning with...

W

# W is for... Witch

# i spy with my little eye. something beginning with...

C is for...

cat

# i spy with my little eye, something beginning with...

# M is for...
# moon

# i spy with my little
## eye, something beginning with...

b is for...

bone

# i spy with my little eye, something beginning with...

# C is for...

## candle

# i spy with my little eye, something beginning with...

# f is for...

# Frankenstein

# i spy with my little eye, something beginning with...

# g is for...
# gravestone

# i spy with my little eye, something beginning with...

# h is for...
# haunted house

# i spy with my little eye, something beginning with...

# b is for...
# broom

# i spy with my little eye, something beginning with...

C is for...

cauldron

# i spy with my little
## eye, something beginning with...

O is for...

Owl

# i spy with my little eye, something beginning with...

# C is for...

# coffin

# i spy with my little
## eye, something beginning with...

# t is for...

## tree

did you have fun and find all of the halloween items?

let's play books created by
© Little Moon Joy Co

Made in the USA
Middletown, DE
17 October 2020

22219789R00024